Finally!

The Manual For

God's Ladies That Lead!

A book every woman needs to read!!

Be Blessed!

"Kameshia"

Jer 29:11

Kameshia Stokes Thomas

Copyright © 2008

Kameshia Stokes Thomas

For additional copies of this book please contact:
Kameshia Stokes Thomas
Email: vthomasfalls@aol.com
Email: ladykameshia5@aol.com

Printed in the USA by
Graphix Network
4104 Colben Blvd
Evans, Georgia 30809
706-210-1000

Acknowledgements

I thank God for using me as a vessel for this book, and for designing me in such a way so that I didn't fit into the wrong grooves.

I love you Lord, and I thank you for your faithfulness in my life and for perfecting all that concerns me. I thank you Lord for sending your son, Christ Jesus!

Every Woman of God needs a best friend, and I want to thank my best friend in the world for encouraging me to write and complete this book. To my dearest husband of 23 years, Pastor Vincent Thomas:

You are my very best friend and I thank you for being my man of God. I follow you because you follow Christ. You make me so proud to be your wife. I love you so very much!

To my children, Vincent Charles, thank you for being such a great role model for your siblings; to my daughter Kristin for being an inspiration to me by being the first published author in our home, and for being the daughter that every mother wants for 17 years. To Michael Carrington for being so kind hearted, patient, respectful, and obedient so that I could have the time to complete this book. I love you all more than you will ever know or understand.

In memory of my parents, Rev. Charles L. Stokes and my mother Mrs. Gwinne Dean Harper Stokes, who taught me to be a woman of God. This was the preparation for becoming a Pastor's Wife. God gave me the greatest parental instructors! To my siblings: thank you for being a part of who I am, without you I would not be who I am today. I encourage you to continue to walk in the pathway that mom and dad pointed out. I am proud of you all.

To my Aunt Ruth Crawford, you are one of the boldest, strongest, wisest women of God that I know. I dedicate this book to you. At age 92, you are a woman with clarity and strength of mind to continue to write books. I sit at your feet and aspire to be like you!

To Dr. Nina Bronner, I have watched your spiritual walk for so many years now. I have always admired your walk as a woman who leads. Thank you for being there for me! Words cannot express my love and respect for you. I love you to life!

To Dr. Bridget Hilliard, I thank you for your mentorship. You created a birthing room with other first ladies for me to learn about things from faith confessions to fun in first lady fellowships! Thank you so much, Dr. Bridget!

To the ladies in the first ladies network, I love all of you. Remember to breathe and keep pushing in the birthing room!

To Thy Will Christian Ministries, collectively, thank you! Being formally Grace Covenant Baptist Church, you were the greatest in support as Rev. Charles Stokes passed the mantel to our Pastor Rev. Vincent Thomas. That baton pushed me to yet another level in my walk as a Woman of God.

To the women of G.L.O.W (God's Ladies of Wisdom), continue being a Woman of Wisdom and 'wow' others for God!

To the Men of Thy Will, thank you for your support. I love you all dearly!

To Lady Natalie Earl, thank you!

Table of Contents

Foreword

I believe there is something to be said about 'good writing style'. An even larger weight is valued on getting the message across to your readers. In fact, if a good teacher is measured by what her students are able to learn, absorb and retain, then Lady Kameshia is wealthy in her domain.

I had the privilege of knowing her parents to whom she references with daughterly affection. Kameshia articulates wisdom that is a gift from God to the reader.

As you read this 'manual' you will find yourself in her kitchen chatting over a stack of pancakes or tea cakes. As a man, I realize how intriguing it can be, trying to understand what goes on in the mind of a woman of God. I have always wanted to know exactly what the day to day operations were about in dealing with ministry from their perspective. Kameshia breaks it down with her crisp sense of humor. Though I had to chuckle, I also remembered the treasured wise walk of her mother. Kameshia passes this wisdom to you in her pancake-style personality. It's good reading, good teaching, great rule of thumb, it is the manual for every lady that leads. Good, anyway you slice it!

C.T. Vivian

Introduction

Whew! Finally! Someone wrote a manual for the ladies who LEAD!!! Have you ever caught yourself saying, 'There is no manual for this job!? Yes, there is! The manual was always in the Bible! Yes, I found ALL of the answers RIGHT THERE! What I have done is consolidate this into a manual that you can refer to specifically on the topic of being a lady who leads.

Of course, FIRST of all, the bible teaches us that '[We] shall be a lad[ies] forever' Isaiah 47:7. So, your questions along with instructions are right here, God given from His Word.

How can every Lady always be a leader? When she is a Woman of God, of course. Only in Christ of course! What I want every woman of God to get out of this book is the fact that Women of God are leaders in their domain.

You may be a homemaker, CEO, school teacher, secretary, manager, cook, wife of the president or government official, or wife of the man of God who is a minister or Sr. Pastor. Regardless of your profession, if you are a woman of God, you are the First Lady of YOUR domain!

I certainly do not mean to demean the Elect Lady who is designed to be a Pastor's Wife. We are certainly women who are set aside to be held to a very high level of accountability and responsibility.

However, shouldn't all women of God have the same character and walk?

The responsibilities are different, but the walk of who we are in the Lord should be the same. Otherwise, we wouldn't be teaching and trying to role model the way every woman of God is to walk in the church. Most women admire their first ladies. In the home, the family admires the mother/wife; in the corporate world the woman of God who is CEO should be admired and respected in that same light. That light is Christ in every woman who loves the Lord.

This is a book that should help not only the First Lady to lead in the church, but also every woman who is First a lady of her domain. It is a book written for the woman who wonders what the first lady is thinking. Here it is first hand. She is a woman much like you with a high calling to live the life she preaches, teaches, and sings and role models every day.

I find it hard to believe that every woman of God does not feel some where in the core of her being that she too wants to be a first lady who leads.

She wants to be important to SOMEONE! I want you to know that if you feel that way, it does not have to be out of selfishness. It is because your assignment on earth is to be special and important to God. He has a special and particular assignment just for you! No one else can achieve the successes that are specifically designed for you the way that YOU are called to do it!

Some women know long before they are even found by their husbands that they will be a first lady or a lady who leads; however, they don't understand how they see that life with no groom in sight.

Allow God to prepare you to lead. If you cannot maintain mere friendships, how can you lead other women to do the same? If you are a woman who does not like to do the girl thing, how can you encourage other women to maintain friendships and marriages?

God is doing a great work in you right now as you are reading this book. Go ahead, read from cover to cover or skip around first. Read the middle or jump in there like some readers and see what the end is going to be first. It does not matter. The fact that you took the time to read the introduction means that you are hungry for every word and piece of information that God has for you!

In this book you will find some huge questions and concerns and you will also find some small things that may seem insignificant, but may truly matter in dealing with the body of Christ. Sometimes in trying to be a good leader we offend and do not realize it, what then? What do you do in the natural to fix it, and when should you just let it go? Go on and study! Bishop Dale Bronner once said, "I am convinced, that you don't get what you want, you get what you prepare for."

In this book, you are going to find information that will equip you. You will also find some general questions that are asked by First Ladies and women who lead from all over the United States.

I am a preachers kid, a child who is a product of parents who were in ministry all of my life. I saw the ups, the downs, the debris and the blessings that cause me to be the woman of God that I am today. My parents seemed to do it right. They did the best they could with the information they had at the time.

We live in a new generation, and we will build on what we already know of course, but the Word of God never changes. It is the same today that it was yesterday. Let's see what God has to say about the life of Ladies who Lead!

Preface

This book is written especially and most exclusively for ladies who are married to a Senior Pastor, Minister, or a man of God!

This book is written for the single woman who is a good thing, that will be found by her man of God.

This book is written for the woman who is the first lady of her domain, her home or her company!

This book is for the young lady who watches her mother and wonders how she does it all in such grace!

This book is written for any man of God who wants to know what she goes through in order to always be a lady who leads!

This book was written just for YOU!!

The Woman of Influence!

Exactly Who Is She Anyway?

Have you ever wondered why women are so intrigued and influenced by the First Lady? Could it be that every woman of God has a bit of First Lady in them?

The Bible instructs the older women to advise the younger women; "...They can train the younger women to love their husbands and children, to be self-controlled and pure, to be busy at home, to be kind, and to be subject to their husbands, so that no one will malign the word of God" (Titus 2:3-5 NIV). This means there is a role and a responsibility for women of wisdom to impart their wisdom to other women. Women of God can do this, because we're equipped with the ability to influence through the power of God.

In this light, I think we should understand that

we are walking in royalty as women of God. I am not just speaking to pastor's wives. God gives the First Lady an assignment over her domain. Your domain may be the government as the First Lady / wife of the President of the United States. Your domain may also be over your home, as first lady of your household where you actually reign as queen with your king.

The pastor's wife has additional responsibilities, but I believe the operative word here is additional. All women of God are Royal! Jesus is King of kings, which means there are kings on earth that Jesus is King over! This is awesome royalty for believers.

Think about it. When we were little, many of us dreamed of being a queen or a princess. We dreamed of being a mommy! Remember playing house? It was in our spirit to want to have the pretty roles in play-life. These women were always beautiful in our minds. As we got older the idea of really being a real princess or queen began to be slim in the natural. We began to look into modeling and acting. Many women deeply desire to be beautiful, royal and unlike the average lady.

What about being the president YOURSELF? You can become the First Lady President of the United States. Don't underestimate the plan of God for your life! If it is your assignment, then walk in it with the boldness and fullness that God has placed inside of you!

Regardless, I think you get my point here. Somewhere deep inside, we KNOW there is a greatness as a woman that we just have not tapped into to the core. I remember watching my mother who was a Pastor's wife. She was admired by so many. She was literally KNOWN locally for being an excellent First Lady. At the time, I was silly, comical and not taken very seriously by many. But, inside ... I KNEW... I knew I was going to be a preacher's wife. I didn't have the nerve to say it to anyone. I thought people would laugh. I thought my sisters and brothers would have a field day with that! I am from a large family and if you know about large families then you know the teasing can either make you stronger or cause you to be a nut. I could be a nut at times, but it was a way for the little princess to get the attention she so certainly deserved.

I didn't mean to be self absorbed; I really thought I was just having fun. But, as I got older I realized that some of it was that I was not a good fit for some average things. A lot of times, I was like a square peg in a round hole. I grew to be ok with that.

It is an awkward feeling to know you are royalty and no one can see it but you! Are you feeling more and more like that nut case you know?

I learned that when God gives you a vision of something in your life, and no one sees it but you, it is not that you are crazy or imagining something that is impossible or not true. If no one can validate this but you and you can clearly see this picture in your spirit, then couldn't it be that God showed it to you and didn't show it to anyone else, because He only needed YOU to believe it for now? You have to give God a chance to set up His divine order for His Will in your life.

I KNEW I was going to be a first lady; I could FEEL and see it! Yet, I didn't want to be a first lady. I knew from watching my mother all of my life that it was a lot of hard work. I saw that there were aspects of that position that were not always pretty.

I had no idea why God kept placing that in my spirit and to tell you the truth. The fact that I was afraid to tell anyone about it, made it easier for me to just try to ignore it. I went back and forth with it. I knew it felt too natural for me to deny. However, the idea of having responsibility to that magnitude was frightening. This is why so many people run from the ministry. If you truly understood the magnitude of what was in store, you could not in your right mind say, "I cannot WAIT for that to happen."

So, I went away to college and God showed me the man who was to be my husband before I met him. HEY... he did not look or act like a preacher at all! In fact, he was quiet and soft spoken. His church met about twice a month and if he missed a beat he didn't even go then!

When I met him, his first words were, "Are you ready to be mine?" I was thinking, "This is the cutest little old fella." I am going to introduce him to my sister. Well, she didn't want him and he didn't want her. At some point, God brought the dream back to my remembrance and at some point, I KNEW this man that I was in love with was my husband. (How in the world could I be married to him and be a first lady when he was not a minister? I saw no indication of it in his people skills. So much for this vision of being a Pastor's Wife. Maybe I missed God on this one, I was not LOOKING for a preacher anyway. I did not really desire to be a First Lady, remember? It was just something really profound in my spirit that felt natural. So, if I missed God on that, well fine... but I sure thought God meant for me to marry a minister!

Ok...almost 20 years later, God calls him to the ministry! WHAT?! I thought to myself, how is he going to preach when he does not TALK to people?

God began moving and working. Before I

knew it, my husband was in the pulpit preaching. I asked him, " Honey... do you think one solid hour is a bit long for a sermon?"

He said, "WHAT? Was it really an HOUR?"

I said, " yes, dear." I was thinking that God must be cracking his side laughing at ME! Who'd a THUNK my husband would have so much to say? So much for being quiet! I wanted to share this with you, because I have met some women who I believe know they have a call on their lives to become a first lady. They cannot explain it, and they know that not many people can see them through God's eyes.

In this book, I want every woman to know how very special she is in God's eyes. It is my belief that we don't have to be taught how to be a First Lady at all. We are all already walking in royalty when we know who we are in Christ! The assignment is to be Christ-like anyway!

Christ had so much influence over the entire world that we are still talking about Him today! When the time comes and God sends the king He has for you, you will not have a lot of changes to make because you are already living scripture! Really, I have seen so many women making such an effort to LOOK Holy by pulling their hair back in what they use to call "a holy ghost snatch back." They would not wear make up and then oil their faces really good to LOOK ANOINTED. They would stop wearing jewelry and believe that even a love song to celebrate the love they have in their marriage is just considered too secular.

When you practice Christian living and make it your true lifestyle, you will become a woman of influence. You will already understand balance, your purpose. There will not be a great difference in your life as a Christian Woman and your life as a First Lady or the lady who leads in other areas of her life. Your character and the way you carry yourself will remain the same. We are "the salt of the earth." (Matthew 5:13) As Christian women, we should possess a flavor that no ordinary woman has! If you are feeling a little different in your circles, stop trying to fit in. God made you different, because he has an assignment that only you can work! You will have to operate in your God given power of influence in order to get things done!

One lady was bragging and being arrogant when she told my mom that the man she was to marry had to fit her list of qualifications. He had to look like this, talk like that, and his portfolio had to be this and that. My mother just listened and when the lady left my mom said, " Kameshia, I think she thinks more highly of herself than she OUGHT." I said, "huh?" My father said, "... that means...she is looking for a king and she cannot find him because the king is looking for a queen." I said, "ohhhh."

You see when you are already walking in Royalty the king can recognize his queen!

Ladies, I don't mean to minimize or make light of the role of a first lady, she has an awesome assignment of being responsible for an entire church/flock. He is the shepherd and protects the sheep, of course.

However, the characteristics of the king in your life should be the same as a pastor. Your king should be a man of God who has integrity, who will lead you as he follows Christ. He should feel compelled to protect you. In this light, you are his first lady in your castle. You, my dear lady, are the queen of your domain. Your walk should be one that is so amazingly different that it will influence others. The power of influence in your walk will cause women all over

21

to recognize you as royalty. They should look at you and see God in you! You have His DNA; you should favor your Father! Think about it. If you favor your Father as a single woman, the Bible says, "He who finds a wife finds a good thing!" (Proverbs 18:22) This means he will find you. You don't have to go hunting down a preacher/minister. You don't have to run after a man/date.

Influence is a God given power placed in women for a specific purpose. To draw others in so that we can lead them to Christ. When we operate in this power, we soar! The procedure for using this power is to see yourself through God's eyes, and then to be who you are. Allow God to set things up for you according to His Will / His assignment on your life!

You will NOT have to marry several times to several men if you learn to listen to God. You will recognize your king when he is in your presence, and he will recognize you.

On the next few pages you will find questions for Ladies that lead. If you are a woman of God with an assignment to be a helpmate to a man of God. You are the first 'leading' lady over the domain to which God has assigned you. Congratulations on accepting the assignment! Did you just discover that the first lady in your husband's life and his domain is actually you?

Questions About The First Lady

My very first spiritual mom was my mother, Gwinne Stokes. As I said earlier she was an exceptional First Lady who was very wise for her years. She taught me so many things. In my walk as First Lady, I am finding that she reared me as First Lady material by making sure that I was a believer and lived a Christian life as best as she knew how. That is all it took! She didn't teach me how to be a First Lady. She taught me how to be a lady of influence and a woman of God. When I ended up as a pastor's wife, the difference was basically in the responsibilities, not in my lifestyle. My lifestyle was already that of a Christian. That was enough for my husband to be able to notice and recognize his queen.

At some point, I realized God wants us to

know that all women are royalty in His eyes. He wants us to instruct the younger women on how to walk in this royal influence.

That is when I was led to write a book that would help any woman of God who strives to please Him. This is really the common thread. We all want to please God. Female believers who want to please God are women of faith.

(Hebrews 11:6 "for without faith, it is impossible to please God.)

Throughout this book, I will share questions that many women want to know. I pray that some of your questions are addressed as well. I am sharing what worked for me and what seemed to work for my mother. Ultimately, we all should understand that when God speaks to you, you have to 'Do You'! I wish you the same happiness in your God given assignment with your husband, or in your single state as you wait on God for more revelations. In the meantime, be aware of your influence that causes intrigue. It is who you are that is the power within you! Use it to glorify the Lord in your walk as a Lady who leads!

1. **Is it true that every woman who is married to a Pastor is called to preach also?**

Understand that the two of you are one. If there is a calling on one, there is a calling on the other. Now, as to what that calling is, only you will be able to figure that in your talk with God. Others may be able to confirm what God has already placed in your spirit. If you are called to preach, God will certainly let you know.

Some First Ladies are called to sing or handle the music ministry. All first ladies do not have the same calling. However, you must remember we are all called to minister even with our mouths closed. People are constantly watching us. In this way, we are ministering even when we do not realize it! This is why you have to make sure your walk is that of a Christian woman. There are some things that will come naturally just because you love the Lord.

There is a way to even wear the latest fashions, and be age appropriate in your attire. This ministers mountains of sermons or lectures without one word.

Think about the young girls that don't always have a mother as a role model. They have been known to walk up to a First Lady and say, "You are so pretty... I want to look like you when I grow up!"

Yes! You minister in the way that you carry your self as well as the way you dress: In a spirit of excellence! I do not claim to be a fashion queen but for some reason my husband goes on and on about how he loves the way that I dress! He thinks it is so classy! I do not like to shop at all, but I have learned to get to know the free personal shoppers in the department stores and that has helped tremendously. Yes, there are actually women like me who could care less about the mall.

I heard my spiritual father talk about how much he loves his wife, Dr. Nina. Other women admire her walk in the Lord and are influenced by it.

Other women admire her also and her determination to demonstrate a spirit of excellence in so many areas of her life.

I grew up singing; I was a soloist and sang with my family in a family group.

Dad called us The C.L. Stokes K.D.s because all six of us had the same initials. My father could sing amazingly well. I pulled my weight in singing but at some point my sisters began to grow and blossom with their voices! It was clear they were anointed to sing exceptionally well. As I got older, I did not solo as much and did more background as my sisters matured more in their own ability to sing.

My husband asked me to take over the music ministry for him and lead praise and worship. I thought that was a huge responsibility for some one more qualified, and I felt that we just needed to wait on God to send us this magnificent musi-cian.

I just could not see myself doing that! God shows me a lot of things, but THAT was not one of them. Where in the world did my husband get the idea that because I can hold a note or two it means I can serve over a praise team? I mean really, isn't it my job just to wear a hat and sit on the second pew on the right hand side and smile?

However, no one else was able to lead praise and worship in our ministry right then either. One Sunday my husband needed to praise God badly. He began to sing, and he belted out a note. I am sure the note was NOT on the keyboard! I realized he was making an awful attempt to sing praises to the Lord. I am sure it was a sweet sound in God's ear but not in mine. My hair stood on my head, and I threw my hands in the air! I am sure others thought that I was in grand praise. However, I was praying and answering my temporary calling from God to sing His praises and lead us into worship! I told God, "I Surrender ALL!" "Yes, Lord, I will get up off of the pew and help in the music ministry." The next year I found myself at the Church Strategies Development Conference, that we usually attend in Texas. I skipped the First Ladies workshop because it was going on at the same time as the music ministry workshop.

I was studying to show myself approved! It was in that workshop that I realized the bigger picture. It was soooo not about me and my ability. It was about the flock my husband was over!

They needed to know what praise and worship was about! I was sooo worried about the wrong thing.

My husband did not let my disobedience to him stop him from praising God in song! My opinion was just that, my opinion. He was not singing to me; he was singing to God! You see, the reason I didn't see my assignment as praise and worship leader is because I am not the Senior Pastor. God gives the vision for the church to the Senior Pastor not to a committee and to the First Lady. I learned that when we submit to authority/order we are much more organized and flow better in obedience to God's plan.

What I learned also was that God will anoint you to do what needs to be done until He gets the qualified person to listen to the set up, be obedient and take their rightful place in the ministry! I would be just fine until he sent some one to do a better job. I held up our music department, be-cause I was not being obedient to the authority and headship God placed in my life as my pastor and husband. Someone else may be hesitating to say yes to God as well. I am also ordained and equipped to minister and help my husband if I ever need to stand in his stead or just help him when God tells him to use me in that light. I am equipped and ready. But, by no means do I con-sider myself an additional Sr. Pastor. Someone once said that anything with two heads is a mon-ster. That sounded pretty precise to me.

I am called to minister, but my husband is sen-ior pastor. Although, I Co-Pastor with him, I never ask him to let me bring the Word. My job is to help him. This is my assignment. He knows how he wants me to help him in ministry. I am not sure what the future holds, but I have always believed as Bishop Bronner says, that our talents will make a way for us.

If I am led to write a message, I do just that. Then, when my husband asks me to minister, I at least feel prepared that God has given me a Word. Even if it changes, I am prepared either way God directs me to go.

Does God ever wake you up in the morning and place a word in your spirit? Right it down! It may be words to a song, a message or a poem. Sometimes that is just a good time for God to reveal some things to you without your daily distractions.

Ultimately, you have to be sure about what God is saying to you about your walk according to His Will. No one can answer your call for you. That is between you and God. If He calls you, you will know it. He has His ways, and His ways are not your ways.

(Isaiah 55:8-9) Early in our ministry, God would wake me up in the wee hours when it was quiet and speak clearly and profoundly to me. I have learned to listen now at other times of the day; however, the wee hour is certainly a great time for me to spend with God talking. As a married woman with children, my distractions are eliminated at that time of morning that God chooses to wake me up. Continue to talk to Him about clarity on exactly what area YOUR particular calling is in.

The answer is "no." All first ladies are not called to Preach, but all first ladies are called to MINISTER as all Christians are called to minister as well. Not always to "preach" but always to minister.

My husband has so much faith and dedication! He stepped out of his lane on faith and had to move in my lane, because I was being stubborn and thinking about me and what folks would say if I could not get it right. I was not obeying God by submitting to the headship He had given me. I had in MY mind what a First Lady is supposed to do. I figured they would look at me like I was looking at him. But we need to understand it is really about bringing others into the presence of the Lord through worship. A First Lady is a helpmate to her husband! She does not have to be labeled as a preacher, evangelist, homemaker, mom or psalmist. She is called to help and that is in any area she is assigned to help! God will anoint her in certain areas more than others as He does with any Christian! Let me share this though, since I am talking about my husband's voice, in print. Since that time he had someone work with his voice, and he is better. He sings so well, I was led to hand him the microphone one Sunday, and he did a great job! Everyone went into even more praise when they witnessed that miracle. God can do ANYTHING!

There is something to be said about being submissive and obedient to the man of God, that is for sure. I am amazed at how much easier life can be when I just listen to my king as he follows Christ!

2. Do I have to take gifts that I don't really want?

We all want to encourage people to be good stewards over their money, and not be wasteful.

However, as First Ladies and as women of God, we should live our lives in such a way that our ground will always be fertile and worth sowing into. I think it is a good thing to remember that when someone sows into you, the bigger picture should be that you want them to be blessed abundantly because of that gift/seed. ("Not because I desire a gift: but I desire fruit that may abound to your account" (Philippians 4:17).

The bigger picture is that you are called as a vessel from God to be a physical being in a flesh suit to receive the gift. The gesture really should be from their heart to God. I think if you can use it, and you like it then at that point you have been blessed as well.

At this point you have become a benefactor. You can also enjoy the walk God has for you as well. The gift is for you to do as you are led with it afterwards.

This means that if someone gives you another tablecloth or purse or shoes or …yes money and you see how you can be a blessing to someone else then you are in order to share. I am not saying be thoughtless in 're-gifting'. But I heard Bishop Dale Bronner say that 'we are blessed to be blessing, we are taught to teach, we are comforted to comfort'. So, yes this includes money as well. You can bless someone else with a financial gift that was given to you. Once it is given to you, it is yours to keep. I think it is fine to bless others and not hoard things. We can be a blessing when we are God-led to do so.

It is good to say thank you regardless of whether you like the gift or not. We have to remember that it is not about whether we want or like the gift. It could be that the person needed to sow into fertile ground, and God sent them to you because you would know exactly what to do with it. We have to remember that this gift may be something that is precious to that person; they may consider it a sacrifice to even give it.

If you know for a fact that the person has ill intentions then yes, you may need to discard a thoughtless gift that you cannot do anything with. However, the intentions should be between that person and God. It is not always for us to position ourselves to judge the heart or the gift. My prayer would be that they will reap a harvest from the seed they are sowing.

So, it would not be about whether or not Kameshia liked the gift. It is about the First

Lady/Woman of God praying with and for the person to expect a great return on their seed.

In addition to that, as a child my mother use to say, "When you are always saying, ' I don't like this and I don't like THAT! People may feel like, "Well, she does not like anything I give her; she is so picky, I just won't give her anything at all!" But, when you are grateful, gracious and know how to say thank you then, you never know, one day they may end up giving you something that you really want. Then you will become a by product of that gift and be blessed!

3. How can I rear my children to be good preacher's kids?

While it is certainly a concern that all eyes are always on YOUR children, understand that you are not trying to TEACH them to be preacher's kids. You are teaching them Christian Living. They should grow up living scripture. Again, this is the goal of any Christian family. I wouldn't stress out of embarrassment when you and others discover that they are just as human as the next family. It should be a teaching moment to others that when your child is out of order / disobedient or deciding that they do not even believe in Christ! (This seems to be a popular trend today as a great excuse for young people to indulge in immoral behavior.) Understand that ALL parents want the best for their children, and they want to know what to do when these things happen.

When they see you apply God's principles in the midst of your stormy motherhood, they are encouraged to know this is how to handle that situation according to the Word of God.

4. **How do I protect my children when it comes to dating in the church?**

Dating in the church should not be any different than rules for dating anyone outside of the church. Teach your child how to respect him/herself. When you teach them to surround themselves with certain types of people, this is what they will be comfortable with in their spirit. Like any parent, you want to know as much about their friendships and persons they are interested in as possible because at certain ages, friends begin to have a tremendous amount of influence. The First Lady should rear her children to be Christ-like, selective in being equally yoked, aware of the environment and certainly making sure that all of their associates are believers. Whether they say they are or not, you will know them by their fruits.

We put so much emphasis and even pressure on our children, because we are certainly aware that there are persons who perceive the First Family as more of a status symbol. There are persons who want to be a part of the First Family by any means necessary. This means, god-sisters / brothers / big mama's in the church, and yes, this includes dating.

However, in this day and time there are mom's who actually push their daughters to date your sons specifically for status purposes.

Understand also, there are great Christian families who have children that are what society calls a great catch! All of these families are experiencing the SAME thing! The difference is that the Pastor is responsible for these people's spiritual lives! So, as a First Lady we have the responsibility of supporting our husbands as they are leading the sheep. That is pretty much it. As far as the rules are concerned, they are all in the Bible for everyone to follow. The man should be a man of God, known in the gates, the wife should be virtuous, and the kids should praise her. When we have reared children according to the Word of God, and the man of God is called to preach you won't have to change your lifestyle or the way your children date.

They will discern the person that is right for them. The Word works for all of us!

5. **What should a First Lady do when she is feeling too tired to be upbeat all of the time?**

Dr. Bridget Hilliard used a term that I just love. She said, "We are the only ones on the planet whose contents are greater than the container." (1 John 4:4) Greater is He that is in you, than he that is in the world.

We all get tired; it is not just a First Lady thing. As women we really do take big bites, and we wear so many hats of responsibilities. We get so caught up being busy. We try to fix so many things ourselves that we just get tired in our spirit, like everyone else.

There was a time when I just didn't do the girl thing very well. I was really comfortable at home with family. My family knew me, and I could talk and not have to preface anything before I opened my heart. They just knew. God showed me that as women we really do need each other. There are some things we can share with each other, and we don't have to preface it with anything. I can talk to another woman and say something like, you know, fibroids are not something I am just going to accept as a part of my life! Most women know exactly how that is affecting my life. We can pray, and I don't have to explain how much a little thing like that can really tire me out or interrupt my life. I am now enjoying our Women's Ministry. I can see how just getting together sometimes and pouring into each other can really be relaxing.

Now I know that I am a container and when I position myself, other women of God can pour some Word into me and I will be filled with the Holy Spirit through my faith. My cup, my container can overflow if I will be still and allow God to use the sister He gave me in another woman of God.

I am reminded of how even God took a rest. Maybe it's not that He was tired so much, because in every thing He does He sets the example of how we are to function. He sets the pattern if you will. He worked and worked and worked, and to this day we know we must take a moment to just stop before we continue. When we stop, we can take a moment to focus on ourselves and our health.

When you think about it, God established a relationship with Adam before he gave Adam the relationship with Eve or any other human being... before the kids, before other people (we now know that is the church).

So when I get overwhelmed, I try to remember the order He set up. He is first, then family (that means immediate household first, then you, and next your husband, then the kids, then everyone else meaning the church.) When I follow the pattern that God gives us, I can truly say, the order frees me up. I can NOT do for my husband or even for God or the kids or ANY one if I have not taken care of the body and mindset God gave me. I would disappoint God, because I would be trying to give a portion of myself that I allowed to be burnt out and run down. That is not the body/mind that God created. When He gave it to me it was fine and in condition to give and be developed to give some more!

I have grown now to find that I can relax and sleep as I am listening to one of my favorite sermons! Sleeping with the Word of God being poured into my spirit has become one of my favorite ways to relax. I will listen to ministers who have a relaxing tone yet profound words of wisdom. It is great for the First Lady to take some me time and rest. It allows you to be able to have the best you: a healthy container with valuable contents. Your husband will LOVE the way you prance around in your strong, attractive, healthy container filled with such valuable contents! What a gift for your family and church members. A well rested ready to serve container!

6. **How can I let members know how to do things for me with a spirit of excellence? I really believe they mean well from the heart. They are just not organized.**

More important than doing things for you in a spirit of excellence, would be to make sure that all things are done in a spirit of excellence for God. By doing this, you will be covered in excellence as a woman of God, a first lady of your domain. One good way to send clear messages to others is to always be yourself. People have a tendency to treat you according to how they see you. If you want to be treated in an excellent way then people need to be able to see excellence in your character and in your knowledge. God has given us everything we need to be able to live in excellence in every situation. God does everything in excellence! This is the pattern we strive to adopt and live by. When you walk in excellence people of excellence will recognize you and will be drawn into your presence. Either because they see something in you they would like to become, or you have a presence about you that they are accustomed to. Either way, your excellent spirit will manifest itself among those persons that are close to you. They will take notice of how you do things and the way you love to have things done. It is a teaching moment for them, they gain knowledge, and it also keeps you on your toes as well. Of course there will always be times when things will not go as planned. We don't strive to be perfectionists, but certainly to do things in a spirit of excellence will be pleasing to God in all that we do. As First Ladies we are women of God who are the role models for our children, people we mentor, and even friends. It is always a good thing to study and be knowledgeable about many things. Striving to live a

Godly life in all areas is a physical pattern to set for a spirit of excellence. A woman of God lives a Godly life in all areas of her life. This is the best way to ensure your teaching moments.

When you are Godly (this means doing things that please God according to His Word) you are striving for excellence in your home décor, your attire, your attitude, personality, disposition, and even in being a good steward over your money. People will become doers in those areas and not just hearers. This is because God has marvelous glory and excellence!

2 Peter 1:3 says, "By his divine power, God has given us everything we need for living a Godly life. We have received all of this by coming to know Him, the one who called us to Himself by means of His marvelous glory and excellence."

2 Peter 1:5 says, "In view of all this, make

every effort to respond to God's promises. Supplement your faith with a generous portion of moral excellence with knowledge."

7. **Do I have to shake hands with people after Service?**

Being a First Lady is a ministry. Remember, if your husband has a calling on his life you have a calling on your life as well. This calling may be for you to teach, preach, sing, administrate, and today in some churches there are First Ladies who actually co-pastor. Regardless, the First Lady ministers whether she wants to or not, whether she is aware of it or not. God has you in a position to minister to others in your daily walk. Ministering does not end with the sermon.

Pastors are a gift to the church. Usually, a pastor has a heart for people. As first ladies, we help our husbands. There are times when women are hurting and broken hearted about things that are just personal and uncomfortable to share with a male pastor. She may feel led to share with you, so you can pray or minister to her about the concern. A simple handshake or smile can save a life if God chooses to do so.

I had to do an assignment for class in seminary, and my instructor asked me to do a paper on the number 5 in reference to the Bible. In my research, of course I dealt with the number 5 meaning Divine Grace. My favorite definition for the word Grace is "special favor!" God has given us 5 fingers that only He can create, and 5 toes that again only He can create! Just think about that insignia that is with us at all times! When we fold our hands to pray, we can take comfort that we have favor when we speak to God in prayer. When we lay hands on the sick and on ourselves, we have favor in our request for healing! In every step we take, there is favor in our walk! When we approach people, God has given us favor to operate in our assignments with! Just think… when we shake hands with someone, with our 5 fingers in agreement with their 5 fingers we have favor in that union!

This is why we need to be careful about who we associate ourselves with. We have a divine assignment from God! Sometimes, when I visit the church of my spiritual mother and the church of my mentors, I will sit after service is over and just watch them. Because my mother is no longer alive, I long some-times for a mother figure to receive spiritual impartations. I think she was the greatest first lady that ever lived. Since she is no longer here to answer my questions in her walk in the natural, God gave me a spiritual mom and a mentor. If you are not a minister's wife, understand as I said earlier that you are the First Lady of your domain. If God has not already given you spiritual parents, your pastor and his wife should be your spiritual parents. You should watch your first lady in the way she carries herself. She is a wonderful role model in the Kingdom of God. When we are in fellowship after service and outside of the church setting we are being watched. So, we are ministering! I watch my spiritual mom and mentor interact with their members and their husbands. I watch the way they help in the ministry. Those things that I admire, I adopt.

One day I was watching, and I was hurting at the same time. I was remembering how my mother would reach out to women after church and just love on them. At that moment my spiritual mom who has a mega ministry of thousands came over and talked to me. Just as my own biological mother would have done! It was comforting, and I was reminded that this is what I have to do and this is why. I have to reach out and let people know that I care, even with a handshake or a smile.

I realize that not all ministries today are able to do that with mega congregations. But, I do remember one lady who said she was a member of the nation of Islam. She went to visit a church and the first lady there who has approximately 30 thousand members looked at her and smiled. She was giving away CD's and books free, and she even gave one to her. This young lady today is saved and a first lady in her own church.

It is amazing how God can move in a mere smile. There are some Pastors and wives who are able to shake hands after church and others who are not able because of schedules etc. But certainly, when God presents the opportunity, make sure to keep in mind the favor that can transpire the power of God between you and a child in the Kingdom. Always be ye also ready to minister in anyway and in any moment that God provides for you.

8.   Can a person really be taught to be a First Lady?

Telling someone HOW to be a first lady, I guess you have to have a lot of nerve to do that is what one would say. But, truly, every woman is a first lady in her own right, in her own domain, territory/turf if you will, that God has placed her over.

Again, I do not mean to demean the role of the Pastor's wife, but I certainly want to encourage the Christian woman to know how important she is to God and how important her own work is in the Kingdom as well. The Bible says that as Christians we should be the salt of the earth (Matthew 5:13) This means our lives should have enough flavor in them that we will be known by our very walk. There is nothing bland about being a Christian woman. People should be able to recognize you in a crowd. They should be able to know you have taste! The taste that a woman of God carries in her daily walk with God.

We should be like a beacon of light. Anywhere there is darkness, when we walk in, we should light up a room with a spirit of exhortation, because we have hidden the word of God in our heart. With the Word hidden in our hearts, we will not sin against God. So where there is darkness, if a Christian woman walks in she will light up the room with her presence, because God's Word is radiating with such power from her heart! That is a First Lady; she is a virtuous woman of God!

So, it is the Bible actually that teaches us to be a First Lady! A First Lady should really have all of the qualities you will find in a virtuous woman. Her husband is a man of God, and because he is a man of God, he is known in the gates. Therefore, he has a walk and an assignment and responsibility to be the king over her life while she is here on earth.

When a man loves a woman and both of them love God!

Some people will jump in the middle of the book to a chapter/page that seems the most interesting to them, instead of reading from beginning to end. If this is what you just did, it is ok! It is fine to get out of our box and not do things traditionally! With that being said, let's get to the good part.

When a man loves a woman, that is an operative phrase right? It is what most women desire. That is because there is something God ordained about the relationship between a man and a woman! Miraculous things happen! Awesome things happen! Relationships are so important to God, and so it is important to us. For us to really understand what happens when a man loves a woman, we have to go back to the source in the spirit realm and see what happened there. Let me take you back for a moment.

In the spirit realm, there is a Love that exists that is so powerful. It is beyond our human comprehension. If we can just understand an important portion, we will never be empty or broken hearted for anything. The Love that exists in the spirit realm is one that covers all of the bases in love. This Love is a person and He is God. Yes, God is love!

We must understand first that God is a God of relationships. He has a relationship with the son and a relationship with the Holy Spirit. In that relationship there is order. God is first, then the Son, then the Holy Spirit!

God gave instructions to man before he was placed on earth. In the King James Version, Genesis 1: 25-31 says, "And God made the beast of earth after his kind and the cattle after their kind, and everything that creepeth upon the earth after his kind; and God saw that it was good, and God said let us make man in our image, after our likeness; and let them have dominion after the fish of the sea and the fowl of the air, and over the cattle, and over all the earth, and over every creeping thing that creepeth upon the earth. So God created man in His own image, and in the image of God created he him: male and female created he them. And God blessed them, and God said unto them, be fruitful and multiply, and replenish the earth and subdue it; and have dominion over the fish of the sea, and over the fowl of the air and over every living thing that moveth upon the earth.

And God said, Behold, I have given you every herb bearing seed, which is upon the face of all the earth, and every tree, in the which is fruit of a tree yielding seed; to you it shall be for meat.

And to every beast of the earth, and to every fowl of the air, and to every thing that creepeth upon the earth, wherein there is life, I have given every green herb for meat; and it was so.

And God saw everything that he had made, and, behold, it was very good. And the evening and the morning were the sixth day."

Then, as Genesis 2:7 explains, He placed mankind on earth: "And the Lord God formed man of the dust of the ground, and breathed into his nostrils the breath of life; and man became a living soul." Here God has placed mankind in the flesh suit. Notice, God has employment responsibilities for man before he establishes a relationship in the physical. He establishes a job, first, then a wife, then children and then the church that we now know is the people. Just give me a minute. I am going to get to the part about how we want a man to love us, but I want you to get this, first! It is important that you know the order and principles. When we are out of order we have confusion, and then we don't understand why the man does not love us the way we think we need to be loved.

God made sure Adam had a job and was a provider before he gave Eve to him as his wife. Amazing concept here, but some times we get it backwards. We look for man, and then we go look together for a job so we can eat.

Ok. God set the example and precedence. He loved us so much that before he placed us in a relationship with Him on earth, He made provisions for us first! He created the earth and every element we would ever need in life so we would be comfortable! THAT is LOVE! THAT is God! He wants us to depend on Him, yet He wants us have a sense of independence to be able to function and enjoy the freedom and abundance that He has provided.

When a man loves a woman, he has so much love in his heart for her that he has this yearning desire to take care of her! Don't take this from a man! Of course you are free and have a sense of independence to do anything your heart desires, but don't take that part of the man that is compelled to love you in the way that God told him to love you. You see he is following God's directives. His spirit man remembers the instructions that were given to him in the spirit realm in Genesis, remember? Consciously, he may have no idea as to why he feels compelled to do things for you, but don't mess that up. He is in his glory when he is obeying God, and you have to allow him to love you this way.

Yes, you can still have a job and work, you can still help him, and yes it is fine to make more money if the job pays more, but never forget or underestimate the headship, the order that God has ordained. Your husband is the provider. If he makes more money, that is fine. If he does not make more than you, it is ok too. As long as he is making provisions for you as head of the household, you need to respect that. You will be amazed at the power of love you will have in your marriage when you respect order.

I had control issues, and I felt I needed to be able make sure that things turn out right. They would if I did it or at least controlled it. It was not consciously, but subconsciously, without me even realizing it. There was power in controlling things and circumstances! This physical power enabled me to protect myself from hurt. It made sure things were always going to be ok, if I could control the negatives that life had thrown at me or mine.

Here is what I learned: Submission. Yes, I said it, and I said it with such ease. This use to be a bad word to me. I really don't like to be told what to do! But when a man loves a woman, truly loves her with the love of God, then he will follow Christ. He will love you as Christ loved the church! When you experience a love like that, you will follow your husband anywhere he wants you to follow him!

Now, understand this, Christ loved the church so much He died for the church! He gave His very life! Now, if a man can love you so much that he will follow Christ and give his very life for you, then do you really find it that hard to submit to him? He is willing to follow Christ, and he is willing to die for you and you cannot do what he asks you to do? If he is following Christ, then he will not ask you to do anything wrong or beneath you. He will live each day as your head, and he will take the hits for you. He will be the one who will have the responsibility of protecting you. Yes, I know you can protect yourself, but picture this: You are doing the things in life that you are passionate about; you don't have to be interrupted, and you can focus because your husband has your back. He is protecting you as he walks in front of you. Yes, he walks in front of you, not beside you! When Satan throws his darts, both of you are targets at the same time, if you are beside him!

However, if your man of God is in front, he takes the hits first and deals with the satanic force. You may never even know what he went through in his walk for the day! So, when he comes home, we follow him to make sure that though he may have endured hurt for us during his working day, he can be assured to have peace in his home. That is why we have to support our husbands and be that help meet that God called us to be! If you are ministering to thousands as a Woman of God, and your husband is pastor of your church and he has a few hundred, he is still your covering. You are to still recognize him and give him honor. He has a huge responsibility!

What am I saying? When a man loves a woman, truly loves her, it is because she allows him to love her. She relinquishes that controlling spirit! She gives the control to

God, because her husband is following Christ!

I had to work with another first lady once, and I noticed right away that she had a strong personality and a controlling spirit. God showed me that if one of us did not submit to the other then there was going to be confusion. Ephesians 5:21 says, "Submit yourselves one to another in the fear of God". That means there are times when we have to yield to one another in certain situations. When God revealed this to me, I knew that I was the one who had to submit to her in the project we were venturing into. I was fine with all of her decisions and did absolutely everything she wanted me to do.

When I made the decision to do that, I suddenly felt empowered. But, it was a different kind of powerful feeling than in the past when I had to have the control. In this instance I was so secure in who I am in Christ that I did not feel the need to be in control of anything. I knew that God was the one who was really in control, and He would look out for me as well as for the other first lady. That kind of powerful feeling was one that came as a result of submission.

You see, when I submit to the proper authority, I am understanding that God is in control. When I understand that God is in control, I can feel secure that all will go well according to the plan of God. Of course, God has my best interest in mind. This caused me to have a more confidence because I knew God was going to handle things. In this confidant walk, I don't have to flinch at adversities, because I know God is in control. NOW you are talking power here. This is the REAL, TRUE power! That is an awesome power to flow in, knowing that God is in control and He always on your side!

It put my dominant persona and control issues to rest. When I put these things to rest, I was able to allow my man of God to love me as God planned. Now, I can allow him to provide for me, and I can still have my career/profession to do as I please. I can become a writer, an actress, a real estate agent, an administrator, the president of the United States if I want to! I know that my man of God will protect me, because he is following Christ. Furthermore, I know that he loves me enough to die for me. I walk in confidence that God is in control and all is well.

Let's see, when a man loves a woman he will follow Christ; he will provide for her; he will even die for her! I had some silly issues holding me back because I didn't like to be told what to do. Let me tell you something. If Kameshia can submit, anyone can!

A man can love a woman when she allows him to love her the way God intended. If we interfere with that, it takes away some of his manhood. Then you are dealing with a man that is not all God planned for him to be. When we understand the order and the directives that are given to him, then we will know when a man loves a woman, there is power involved, beyond what you could ever imagine.

…And Both of them Love God,

The Bible says that when two of them are joined together, God will be in the midst! The Bible also says that the two will become one flesh. God is love. So, when BOTH of them love, there God is manifested in the midst! When both of them love, there is God. When two people are joined together in matrimony, love is born. God is RIGHT there! When both of them love God, something miraculous happens. They begin to connect, spirit to spirit. A love happens that simply cannot be explained.

The First Lady is a woman who loves the Lord. Her husband becomes a man who follows the King of kings. He loves the Lord as well. The First Lady reigns in the Kingdom as a Woman of Strength. God has equipped her to be able to endure, because she is one with the king. She is not above problems issues and concerns. She has them as any other woman does. She is righteous at heart and because God hears her prayers, the First Lady becomes more than a conqueror. After all she is a Woman of God!

The children are not better or greater than the children of any other Christian. They will be challenged with the ugly things that life has to offer in the natural as well as the natural blessings. The difference is that the children are products of both the man and the woman loving God. This combination of power and influence is one that is God given when we live the Word. The children will walk in their destiny because they are submitted to the First lady, the woman of God, who is submitted to her King, who is submitted to Christ the King of kings! Sure, children can be reared wonderfully in a single parent home, because God can do anything but fail. He can raise wonders in really dysfunctional situations. However, if we actually follow the plan of God for our lives, we will understand that God meant for us to live in joy. This type of joy is manifested when the man and woman love God. We produce children of God, and we are equipped with twice the amount of ammunition needed to defeat satanic attacks on our lives and the lives of our children.

Man was placed first and given instructions. He was empowered by God to be able to function as a man of God to protect, provide and unconditionally love one woman for the rest of his life. He is equipped to want, to give and to share with one woman everything that God has given him authority over.

Now, combine that with a woman who also

loves God. She is also empowered. She has authority over and is responsible for every human being walking on the planet when they get here. God equips her to be able to physically see to it that the earth is populated through her body being in care of the creation in action! That is a lot of power, responsibility and a lot of influence. She has to be careful about every morsel that goes into her mouth. She must use wisdom about substances in her surroundings. She is so precious as she cares for the creation in action (pregnancy), and God gives her supernatural and dynamic influence that will affect that creation for the rest of its life!

Now, combine the power of the man of God and the power of the woman of God. When BOTH of them love God, you have a protective, providing, dynamic love that al-

lows you to be created to do what God has assigned you to do! There are no other entities
on earth that have responsibilities to this magnitude. When both of them love God...they
can do ALL things!!!

9. **My 18 year old child suddenly let me know she does not believe in God anymore. This is devastating and embarrassing to us. Being in ministry makes it seem worse. What do we do?**

The Bible says that the seed of the righteous shall be delivered. You have to believe this. It is, after all, according to your faith, so hold on and do not give up. You are in this to win, so fight a good fight!

You have done your job. Your child is now 18 and old enough to make his/her own decisions. I have heard Dr. Bridget Hilliard say so many times that the ungodly choices our children make have no reflection on our righteous commitment. When you have reared your child according to the Word in the way that he should go, you must trust that God's Word will not return to Him void!

Love him/her! Love them! Role model your Christian walk! This ministers to others that this is the way we handle this type of situation with our children. Dr. Bridget Hilliard says to remember we are in this win!

10. **I never heard any audible voice calling me to preach or to be a pastor's wife. Why didn't I have this 'burning bush' experience like others?**

God does not speak to everyone in the same way. Exodus 33:11 says, "And the Lord spake unto Moses face to face, as a man speaketh to a friend." If you were not called to be Senior Pastor and your husband was, then you may not hear the same thing. You do have different assignments. Your job may not be to pastor in the capacity of Senior pastor. Your job as a First Lady may be to help your husband instead of heading up a ministry. God will speak to some people in their spirit, to some it may be through day or night visions. Sometimes, God speaks to us through people, but do not be confused because your experience is not the same as someone else's. The point is that you are to be sure of your calling and stay in your lane. If you were called to sing and not minister through sermons then do as God has called you to do. Be open for Him to use you when he wants to. Don't worry about the labels of evangelism, pastor, minister, first lady, apostle etc., just do as God leads you to do. If you minister to one person or to one thousand, it should not matter. Either way you should only say what God trusts you to say in His word. Don't be intimidated by the podium, use it to rest your Bible on when you are ministering, whether you have 10 persons listening or ten thousand. Don't get caught up in things that don't matter. The bigger picture is to say yes to God if He whispers, uses a thunderous voice, or your inner spirit. Be obedient. You are ministering by simply sitting on a pew or in the stands of the little league baseball game, because there will always be someone watching the anointing of the Lady That Leads. There should always be at least someone who admires you in some way. After all, you are that beacon light, the salt of the earth. You are a Woman of God, and that makes you a lady who leads in your domain!

11.   I am one of those rare women who do not enjoy shopping. Yet, I want to present myself in a way that will represent God in the Kingdom as a First Lady. How can I do this when I don't like to shop?

Analyze your reason for not wanting to shop, and you will come up with some solutions. If you do not like trying on clothes over and over, just remember this is the age of technology. You can shop on line without trying anything on.

I have a friend who loves to shop. She volunteered to shop for me, and would actually bring clothes for me to choose from. Then, I would pay her for the clothes. This was a part time job that she did for women who didn't like to shop or didn't have the time.

If your dilemma is that you are just not sure about your taste and what is up to date, know that there are some department stores that offer personal shopper services free of charge. They assist you from head to toe, and even help with jewelry and make up suggestions.

There is simply no excuse for a woman of God not to be able to keep herself up in an attire that allows her to walk in a spirit of excellence!

12. **My husband is doing it all himself! I am tired because he is tired. He does not designate much and has to have his hands in everything all of the time. How can I get him to see the damage it does to both of us and the family?**

In my father's day, they did that sort of thing in many churches. Sometimes it is a result of something happening in the ministry. at some point and there is a feeling that develops that in order for things to be done right, they must do them all their way. You are right. This can be quite taxing on you as a first lady and your family as well. In the home, stress can be contagious if it is continuously allowed to get out of control.

Today, with a church going up on almost every corner, there is a need in the Kingdom for the advice and wisdom of those pastors that have experience in the area of helping others in ministry. For those persons who are not pastors, leadership, lay leaders and laypersons, your spiritual advisement should come from your pastor. Your pastor and your first lady of the church should be your spiritual parents. Age does not matter in these cases, because God has equipped the man/woman for this particular assignment.

For pastors and First ladies your spiritual parents/mentors should be persons who are placed in your life by God. You should pray and ask God to direct you to the persons who are to make spiritual impartations in your life. This person should be in a place/level spiritually that you desire to go. There is always another level that we need to strive for, and your spiritual parents should be in a position to pour into your life. The pitcher can not pour into a glass if it is on the same level. This is a relationship that should develop in the utmost respect. You should not be common with your spiritual parents anymore than you would be common with your natural parents.

Don't get me wrong spiritual parents are not perfect beings; they are human and subject to human error as we all are. However, they should be persons who are able to speak into your life, so that you will be receptive to sound spiritual counsel. Men will often times listen to each other as women listen to each other. In these relationships when they are developed and respected another pastor may be able to say, "Slow down and remember the order of God. The order is God first, then family, then the church. A reminder from another spiritual source can sometimes solve in simple terms what seems to be catastrophic at the time.

13. **My husband does not believe in "Spiritual Parenting." He does not have mentorship that he wants to talk to about the things we are going through. I feel that I need this help and so does he. What do I do?**

These relationships are not things that need legal documentation. A mentor can be a person that you look up to and who's walk you admire. As Christians we want to make sure that the persons we admire are also children of God. However, if your husband is not receptive to talking to anyone about the things you are up against, then by all means pray that you can have a mother figure in your life that you can talk to, if this is what you feel you need. Women, more than men, have persons in their lives they can get support from emotionally and spiritually. However, if your situation with your husband is of such that he is just not open to this from anyone, know that you always have access to God yourself. God has made a way so that we can get to Him when the natural things and ways of this world are not available to us. Go to God and know that He will perfect all that concerns you and your husband.

Don't forget to ask that God to make your life such a light that your husband would hearken to the plan of God on your lives and move in the direction that God provides.

There is also a wonderful book called, "Ye Have Not Many Fathers" by Dr. Mark Hanby with Craig Lindsay Ervin. I found this book to be enlightening in trying to understand the biblical basis for spiritual parenting. In every Woman of God, there is a First Lady, in every First Lady you will find a Woman of Influence.

In everything that we do we have to envision the bigger picture. We must know that is about so much more than us. We have the ability to influence other women in ways that only a woman can. In our dress, we can exemplify the outward beauty of the Christian woman. In our demeanor and body language, the way we carry ourselves should be compared to a light in the midst of darkness. We should have influence over an entire room that is without the light of God. This is how much our light should shine. Because we have the authority to influence our children from the embryonic state, we have the power of influence to affect every human being on the planet! Women are the first to nurture, the first to influence, the first to introduce a Godly life even if it means watching everything we inhale or eat before a life comes in the world. We are the First for a reason. We are Women of God, Women of influence, we are ladies who lead, and we are certainly First Ladies of our domain!

14. **I pride myself in not trying to be my husband. He is very charismatic when he is ministering to others. I am only me and only a First Lady, shouldn't I be satisfied with that? I cannot compete with him.**

First of all there is no such thing as "Only" a First Lady. First Ladies/Women of God are Women of Influence! You do not have to be intimidated because of his calling/anointing. Know that he is in his lane, and you are in yours. In other words walk in the boldness and the fullness of the plans God has for you. You may sing, or if he is preaching or teaching, maybe God has anointed you to simply 'talk.' It may be something really anointed and profound about your talking that will draw others to Christ. Joyce Myers is a person that I love to listen to. She has an anointing on her life to simply talk, and people are drawn to her, 'chat'. Whatever your anointing is, Do You! You will influence someone in the ways and the path leads to Christ. This should be our main focus.

15. **What happened to so many of our high profile ministers who's marital and other problems that are exposed in public?**

As with any child of God the Bible says, "Many are the afflictions of the righteous: but the Lord delivereth him out of them all" Psalms 34:19) Dr. Bridget Hilliard said in her teaching once that there are 4 reasons that we face trouble:

1. Satanic Attack

2. Challenging times

3. The Call of Ministry

4. Just mean folk: not Satan... just mean folk.

Just because there is a powerful anointing on a man or woman of God that allows them to minister to thousands/world wide and in celebrity circles, this does not mean that they will one day reach a level when they will never have another issue. As women of God / First Ladies, we simply must remember that we are women of Influence. Everything that happens in our lives can be subject to public view. In this light, we have to remember that our ministry is in the way we handle our issues/concerns, not that we don't have any at all.

The way we come out of it will minister to others who are experiencing the same thing. We don't want the world to know all of our issues. Similarly, any other person does not like everyone to know the things they are working on until they have come out of it, or until there is a full testimony of the love of God in our lives. In these cases they are going through this in the public eye, we pray for them as they surface in the manner that God has for their walk.

Again, the thing to remember also is that we

will never reach a level in life when we will never again have any troubles. Each level of trouble comes with a level of faith.

 I love the way Dr. Bynum put it once, " … there is always another level!"

16. I have a lady in my church who is very helpful to me; God showed me that she was to be a help to me in the form of an assistant or armor bearer of some sort. I don't know a lot about this sort of thing. And to tell you the truth, I really feel uncomfortable asking her to do things for me. However, I need the help. I am always thankful that she makes my position as a First Lady so much easier. She told me that God said for her to assist me. I knew this, but didn't know how to approach her with it. Now, that she has come to me with it. How do I get used to having an Assistant, and why is this situation developing for me?

First of all, you may want to read the book called, "God's Armor Bearer", and another great book called "Walking In Your Destiny," by Dr.

Juanita Bynum, as well as, " Your Silent Years", by Bishop Dale C. Bronner.

These books can give you a great understanding of a person's walk when they are assisting some one in ministry.

For some people, this position is only temporary, a passing through season, a step in the walk for their lives. For others this may be a permanent position. Regardless of the length of time, understand that this is really not about you at all. This person is in a position to serve. For some people, this is a supernatural gift they operate in; for others, it is an assignment for them to assist you at this time. One thing we need to know is that it is really not about us. It is about this person's opportunity to serve in the natural. It is a seed they will reap a harvest from. Ephesians 6:6 says, "Knowing that whatsoever good thing any man doeth, the same shall he receive of the Lord, whether he be bond or free." What you do for others, God will make happen for you!

Remember, you are a Woman of Influence. This is an opportunity for you to pour into this woman of God, who will be by your side closely and frequently. There may be something she needs to glean from you; it could be your articulation skills, your people skills, your walk of integrity, or your walk as a first lady, etc. There are some things that may need to be imparted in her that cannot be taught in one conversation. However, if the person has been blessed with the assignment to assist you, then they will watch your every move when you are together. They will receive impartations from you on a routine basis, even at times when the two of you may not realize it. Thank her by blessing her from time to time, since this is not a paid position. Be God led on the things you do for her, and know that your example is one of the greatest blessings that you can sow into her life.

17. **I do not feel that I deserve to be a First Lady. I just don't feel worthy of this position. How do I deal with that?**

Anytime a person has been called to ministry, if they would truly be honest with themselves. They would admit somewhere inside they really do not feel worthy of telling others how to live their lives. This is because we are human. This means we are subject to human errors. When we think of the assignment from God, we think we have to be perfect in order to carry this assignment out. This is simply not true. Look at the persons God used in the Bible for ministry. They all had issues of some sort. Being a First Lady is a calling from God as well. It does not matter if you married a minister or if your husband was called after marriage. If you are a woman of God and your husband is a man of God, then you have a mission/ assignment. All Christians may not preach/pastor, but all Christians have a responsibility to live their lives in such a way that it will witness through example of your lifestyle/walk in the Lord or through your testimonies, teaching, witnessing, and singing.

As a First Lady, you have an opportunity to preach the word, sing the word, write the word, live the word, pray the word, and teach the word. What ever calling you have on your life, you are obligated to use that calling to bring others to Christ. Some people actually say no to God or they wait a long time, trying to find the hour of worthiness. It does not come; we never get to the point where we feel worthy of this assignment.

We only get to the point where we trust God. We make up in our minds that our past will not determine our future. That is a testimony in itself. We can move forward in spite of a past we are not proud of, and encourage others to do the same. For those of us who have the courage to say 'Yes" to God, we pray for each other and we strive to make each day one that will be pleasing to the Lord. It becomes a self esteem issue that is rectified through trusting the fact that God will forgive and equip us for this assignment. Walk in boldness; your equipment comes from God Himself!

18. **Now that I am a First Lady, I feel like I am expected to be submissive and wear a hat and sit on the second pew from the front on the right hand side. This is just not me, I don't do hats, and I was called to be in the pulpit. How do I handle these expectations?**

Understand that the Bible says we are to submit to our husbands. You cannot get around the fact that we are to submit to order. This does not mean women cannot pastor, become bishops, evangelists, CEO's, or managers, etc. It simply means that the man (our husband) is the head, and it is his responsibility to submit and follow Christ. His job is to love us as Christ loves the church. Christ loved the church enough to die for us, our husbands have that same responsibility. They are to love us enough to die for us. That is a lot of love. I am a woman who had issues with being told what to do, but in understanding what true submission is really about, I realized that when he follows Christ, it is always a win/win situation for me!

My prayer is for him to always do as God wants him to do in following Christ! My benefits are awesome at that point.

In the Bible, Deborah was a judge. She led men to war, yet she was a married woman. It was her job to tell men what to do; yet, she had a responsibility to lead men to war. It would behoove them to listen to her directives so that lives would be spared.

God is the same God today that He was yesterday. If he needs to call some Deborahs today to go to war or spiritual warfare, we need to be mentally, physically, emotionally, and spiritually equipped to do that. So, in the expectation of being submissive, know that we submit to our husbands. A wife is expected to submit to her husband as he follows Christ. Dr. I.V. Hilliard has a wonderful book with great teachings on this issue. It is called, " Daughters of Destiny." His teachings will show you how to be an awesome woman of God, walking in the boldness and fullness of who you are in Christ! I recommend it highly. If a bold sister like me can understand and walk in submission to her husband, believe me, any woman who is a true believer can do the same thing.

As far as the hats are concerned, and where to sit in the church, you have to DO YOU! God made you the unique person that you are, so that you will be able to fulfill the assignment that was designed especially for you. You have to be yourself, the way God made you.

My mother sat on the second pew, wore hats, and dressed well. She was also an anointed teacher in the school system, and she taught in the church as well. When she was in the pulpit she was called a " Speaker of the Hour." The title does not matter, as long as the word of God goes forth. If you were called to sit in the pulpit instead of the pew in your church, then by all means, sit where you and your husband are in agreement for you to sit. Wear the clothes of the women of today with class and style. Let other women see what a beautiful woman of God looks like. I am sure they will be influenced to want to look like a stylish woman of God too!

19. **How do I handle remarks/comments about my attire and style of living? Do I really want to invite church members to my home? What if they talk about me later? I am thinking I may need to keep my home life private and separate from church.**

Handle the remarks with the wisdom of the Word. Always use those times as a time to minister. I wouldn't take offense to the remarks/comments, even if a person means it to be offensive. The bottom line is they may not have what you are blessed with, and you may have more than someone else. You know, more than likely there is someone on the planet who has more than you do.

This is a great opportunity to minister and tell them how they can have the same things. You are a First Lady / Woman of God. We are usually blessed, and it is ok to be blessed. Don't feel bad about that fact. You are leading the way to show others how to get what they want. What we all want in the midst of our assignment is abundance, whether it is in love, things, or health. Jesus is fine with that. He said that's why He came, so that we could have life ABUNDANTLY. I think there is a nice way to find the answers from someone who has what you want. However, there are also sarcastic ways of asking. The bottom line is that our Father is rich, and we need to tell everyone about the inheritance He has for His children! The important thing in having the guests in your home is that you are ALWAYS you!! When we are living the Word, we are consistent anyway. Whatever your reaction would be to a person inside of the church, we should have the same reaction in our homes and other places outside of the church. If you are truly a woman of God who practices daily living the Word of God, then you can ALWAYS do you. You will always be great at that and please God.

I would suggest that you be God led in who you invite to your home. Also, make sure the occasion and circumstances are well planned. There are ways to have guests over when you are a small ministry and other ways when your ministry is much larger.

Always be God led in who you invite to your home regardless of whether you are Woman of God who is married to a pastor, or if you are the First Lady over a domain that God has assigned you to outside of the church. There are some common sense tips we need to be mindful of in the natural of course.

However, in those assignments/occasions, when God wants someone to experience a more intimate side of our life, remember Bishop Dale

C. Bronner teaches that we are blessed to be a blessing, we are taught to teach, we are comforted to comfort. In this light, yes we do have times when we share a more personal side of our lives. Just remember, everything we do and say and the way we walk and live ministers to some one else in some way.

When a remark is made, it may be a time to minister and bless them with the wisdom/equipment to be able to get the same thing you have and more! If you are led to share your home, do so. Don't let Satan rent space in your head about remarks!

20. I have noticed that some first ladies view fellowships as some form of competition. How do I deal with that in my friendships with them?

Deal with jealousy the way you would deal with it in any relationship. Walk in the confidence of who you are and do not worry about it. Again, being a first lady does not mean you have to be better than anyone, but it does mean you have a responsibility to role model the life of a Christian woman. When you focus on what God has for you to do in your assignment, you will find you really don't have time to notice jealousy.

21. **Apparently I offended another First Lady, and I didn't realize it. I noticed that she treats me differently now and is a bit stand-offish. I have apologized several times, because I really admire and care about her as my sister in Christ. Yet, she seems to have a problem letting it go. It was truly a misunderstanding. What is worse, is that she will not admit that there is a concern.**

You have several options you can take. First of all remind yourself that the fact that she is a 'First Lady' has little to do with anything. We certainly do not want to put ourselves so high on a pedestal that we think the common concerns of everyday life will not happen to First Ladies or to First Lady friendships. Understand that the way you handle that is the way you will minister to others on how to handle the same situation. So, your job in the bigger picture is make sure you are role modeling.

Also, just because that person is a first lady does not mean that she automatically knows how to carry herself as a first lady. Sometimes it is a matter of her husband being called into the ministry, and she is just realizing that there is a call on her life as the wife of a man of God.

The solutions: You have apologized, now move on. If she is a woman of God, the situation will be revealed to her and matters will be fine. Move on, and do not dwell on it. Do not push her to understand your motives, ROLE model who you are in the Lord.

Continue to be you. Continue to do you. Remember, this is yet another opportunity to influence another woman to see God in you! She will eventually see your heart for who you are.

Understand that she may not be where you are in forgiveness. If that is the case, it is ok. God is patient with you in the areas you need to grow and mature in. Be Christ-like and be patient with her. Continue to pray for her and allow God to work that situation out.

Position yourself to be admired! I was working in the school system once, and I watched a co-worker carefully. I admired how meticulous she was in her attire, and in the way she carried herself. Her articulation skills intrigued me she was so polite. I loved her countenance of control and confidence. Her job became stressful, and she came to me for help because I knew someone in a higher ranking position that could help her. I spoke to the higher ranking person and introduced her so that help would avail if needed. The short story is that the higher ranking person chose for some reason not to help her. My co-worker never spoke to me again. I have no idea to this day what happened. I do know that I made every effort to find out what the problem was, and it was never revealed to me by her. To this day I think of her and smile, because I learned so much about her Godly walk. To this day, she does not realize it, but she mentored and ministered to me at a time when I was clueless about the walk God had for me as a lady who leads. I do understand that God placed me in her life to learn certain things that help me now. I have a picture in my mind of how to handle stressful situations. She left an impression on me concerning her people skills.

Can you see how in this situation, although she may still be angry or upset for some reason, not only did God use her for His glorification, but she mentored me and didn't even realize it. If you have someone who is upset with you, try to look at the bigger picture and the lesson behind it all. If you on the other hand are the one who gets upset easily, or you feel someone dear to you has wronged you, understand that you are role modeling the lifestyle of a Woman of God. That is the bigger picture. Move on, if it is time. It is ok. There was purpose in it all.

22. What is my responsibility to a spiritual mother?

Your basic responsibility to your spiritual mother would be similar to that of your biological mother, but on a spiritual level. You are to pray for her, be supportive, and ready to receive Godly counsel from her if you ask her for it. It is really not complicated. She is one who should be on a level you are striving to be on spiritually. Because of this, there are things you will be able to glean from watching her life.

Also, when God places a spiritual parent in your life, it is for life. Someone else may be pouring into you in any particular or given season, but if you have listened to God then your spiritual parent will not change. Even when you have grown up in a certain church, and you have to leave for your assignment from God. There will always be a place for this woman in your life, even if it means she mentors you from afar.

Your spiritual parent should not be someone who is connected to you because of the way they dress, how much money they have, or because they have a huge name that you can attach yourself to. A spiritual parent should be one that you have a relationship with that glorifies and reflects God.

There is an excellent book called, " You Have Not Many Fathers" by Dr. Mark Hanby with Craig Lindsay Ervin that is a great resource and a great read on spiritual parenting.

23. **I would like to take the women in our women's ministry out to dinner for a special occasion. We are a small ministry, and right now we can afford to do this. Should I take them to my favorite place, or should I allow them to decide the restaurant they would like to go to?**

I think you need to do you. The personality of the membership will favor the leadership. They will follow you, because you feed them what they need most. Some first ladies would rather make that decision because they love to share a part of themselves/personality with others. They live unique lives and love blessing others with their experiences. There are other First Ladies who would prefer to make sure that the ladies in the ministry are dining at their own favorite place that the majority of them choose. It is also a joy learning about the lives of others.

Personally, I am not picky about food, and I can find something I like on almost any menu. I love watching my assistant eat. She prepares for her meal like a director at a symphony! It is quite entertaining. I love watching the differences in people, and I can get exasperated with detail easily. My opinion is to just 'do you'. People love it when you are genuine in the way that you care.

The Royal Walk

In the natural, I have never seen or known of a person of royalty to hurry or scurry. They don't seem to make decisions in haste. There is a timing that is used. There is a time for reflection and meditation on the situation at hand. There is a walk of confidence and profound countenance in each step. The shoes are filled with the essence of who the person is. I learned from my mother to choose my timing in talking to my husband. That same rule of thumb proved to be a good thing in other areas of my life too. I learned that if I took my time, then I could make decisions that were good ones.

Sometimes, I can hear from God and in all honesty, sometimes I don't hear anything. It is those times that I have to pull on the Word inside of me; the Word that God is trusting for me to fall on.

So, you found yourself in the shoes of a First Lady! Remember there is a massive amount of power that is given to the Woman of God. This 'power' is called 'influence'. As with any gift, most especially one from God, be careful and discerning in how you use your gift. As a woman of God, make sure that you know what to bring even in the form of mere conversations to the man of God in your life. You have an amazing amount of influence when you speak to him. He will hearken to your voice before anyone else's voice. The trust he has in the anointing on your life is respected by him. He knows that you will do him good and not harm all of your days together. That is a position to be treasured. Walk in your best spiritual shoes for God, and it is you that God will use to influence the entire planet! The time belongs to you.

It's Your Time!

All of them, every single one of them wanted to be a First Lady. They all gathered around. They were always there. They all knew this man would need a wife and she would be a First lady once they were married. They had in mind how a First Lady should look. So, the make up was explicit, you know, that " finished look" is what they were really trying to achieve.

Of course you know there is a walk. She has to have the walk of one who is married to royalty. This woman would have it all; he had to choose one, so why would it not be me? This is the thinking of women all over the world today. Believe it or not. There are women who seek this position. Think about it: the attention this position seems to be one where the woman wants for nothing. She dresses well, so well that it is really a part of her job to always dress and do everything a step above the average woman. What a job! What a position to have!

So, you can understand why women would swarm around a man who is searching for just the right one. She has to be a step above the rest already; he must be able to recognize her when he sees her. Some of the recognition is in her walk. Does she stride? Is the walk sexy? What is attractive to him about the walk she has? This man was looking for a wife, and everyone KNEW it. So, each time he came around they were all looking their best. They were certain it was in the "look." I mean, after all men are 'visual' beings, right? So, the focus needs to be on how well you keep yourself up.

There was this one woman though, who was oblivious to the desire for some reason. She knew that he was looking for a wife, but she really was not looking for husband. I mean, she had been without parents for a while, and she had a cousin who had reared her. Yet, he was constantly pouring into her. Her walk was one that was pronounced. You see, in her community, she learned quickly that you needed to have a great walk in life. This walk was one that was not determined by the sway of her hips, or the stride of her steps. Most women learn to use that pretty effectively at some point. The walk of this lady was a walk that incorporated wisdom. She had to have that to survive; her life had been rough. She had no idea what her life would be like if this cousin were not a part of it in some way. Having a male figure in a woman's life is vital. It determines what her relationship will be with men in her future. She will depend on what her experiences tell her.

They were all walking, but he noticed her! There was something about her walk! She found herself in the midst of some competition. She didn't really get into the make up, even though it was offered to her. She just wasn't feeling the entire competition thing. Really, she was just comfortable being her self. Star was her name, most referred to her as Esther.

She was chosen. Even though she knew this was a position of greatness, it was not one that she yearned for. In fact, for some reason she found herself in the midst of it all. Everyone was making this huge fuss. She was not nonchalant about it; she was just compelled to be the only thing she really knew to be, herself. What did he see in her? I thought men were visual beings? She didn't have the make up on, and she didn't even bother with the designer perfume. Yet, there was something about this woman, Star, that set her apart from the rest.

Have you ever seen this happen today? You

can watch your weight, wear the latest trend, and your make up will be flawless: you can be the epitome of the perfect female. You know the proper conversations to have with the man. You know you are beautiful, you are told this all of the time, and then he chooses... her? Couldn't he do better than... that? She doesn't even try to compete! Where in the WORLD is her make up anyway? You spend money on Bobbi Brown, Mac, Fashion Fair, Mabeline, Prescriptives, etc., and this chic, is the one he chooses. The one with NO make up!!

This is the thing though, Star was the star of the show and the other women didn't even know it. It was even in her name that she would shine above the rest.

What he saw was a woman who was not in desperate mode; she walked in the confidence of who she was created to be. She was oblivious to being needy. Even though she lacked so much at times that she didn't even have a set of parents to rear her, she was a woman of focus who was destined to become a Woman of Influence and it was all in her walk. It was speaking, saying something, making a statement all in her everyday walk.

She talked, but she was not chatty. She was a woman of focus, a Woman of Influence in the making. This would lead her to be a Lady who Leads!

Speaking of talking, it is really fascinating that she took after her Father in heaven who was just not in a talkative mode during these days. Theologians have their speculations as to the reason. But, in spite of it all, the bottom line is that God did not say one word in the entire book of Esther! He just got quiet. Esther favored her Father. Her talk was not idle, and so when she did decide to speak, people listened.

Star ends up with an assignment that she never imagined would be on her shoulders. The First Lady has to represent other women, and yes, at times, other people. As a First Lady, a portion of her responsibility was to protect her people, the flock if you will. She didn't ask for this job, remember the situation just comes to her attention and she finds herself in a conversation. The conversation is not with God; it is with another man in her life, her cousin. While reigning as Queen/First Lady, Star is submissive to the authority figures in her life. Her cousin was a natural 'spiritual father' figure whom she trusted. Even though she was married, she still trusted him to be truthful with her. She valued the spiritual impartations he made in her life. The one thing that stuck with her though was that he said, " Maybe you were sent to the Kingdom for such a time as this!" Time? It was indeed her time! She was talking to her cousin, but not to God. Oh, she went to God. She prayed; she even fasted. She heard nothing, because God was not talking.

Do you ever feel that way? You know you are special to God, look at the position he has placed you in. You have these benefits of course, but the work is so hard. You are up against so many adversities that you wonder how in the world you were the one who was chosen for the assignment! People literally want you out of the way. They want to get to the king and face it; sometimes, they feel you are just in the way. Yet, you know that it is you who has to do the bulletins initially when the king has no one else; it is you that must take the messages when he is working; it is you that will handle the business of the church the body of Christ, you that must tie up all of the details. You will do everything, set it all up and make a perfect platform for him to speak to the people. It is you that he will bounce things off of, pray with, encourage him, protect his heart and mindset from the trivial things that could worry him. You have the authority over the kids, and when someone you trust brings you an issue that you know could destroy the entire church if he gets this information the wrong way at the wrong 'time,' you are the one to deal with it. You are the one who knows your man, and you have an anointing that can build a man up or tear him down. There will always be an idiot that wants to destroy what God has set up for good. There will always be a demonic spirit that will want you to find a reason not to minister and help your man of God. You don't have TIME for such foolishness as not helping. You have a divine assignment from God to have your husband's back. You are responsible for making sure there is peace at home! He has to make decisions in peace that stem from the home. You have to pick the right time to talk to your husband!

So, you go to God, and you pray. You hear nothing. Not one thing. You see a catastrophic situation in process. You fast, pray and anoint the doors with oil. You pray in your English tongue, and you pray in your spiritual tongues. You meditate to HEAR from God, and He says...NOTHING??

Why would God suddenly get quiet when it is MY time? Any other time in life, God spoke. Jesus even came and spoke to the trees, the wind and the waves! But, when I need God, I have not heard one thing. In fact, at what point did he tell me Himself that I would end up as a First Lady anyway? At what point exactly did I ask for this job? I never asked God to let me lead anyone anywhere! God places me here and says NOTHING? There are no instructions? No manual? No Books out?

It is what we all face, if you are CEO of a company, if you are the manager, if you are the wife and mother of 10, if you are a widow who will pour into other women, or if you are a beautician who has the opportunity to minister to many women daily, you will face a 'time' when you will need to hear from God. And sometimes, He just does not say anything. It is then YOUR TIME. I have found that God gives us a time for everything. (Ecclesiastes 3: 1-8).

There will be a time for you to use your influence, the anointing on your life to have the ability to cause people to see things the way God needs them to see things. Your time will come when you will have to rely on the God in you, the word you have studied. You will have to rely on the Holy Spirit who is always with you. Rely on your ability to encourage your man of God that he can do ALL things through Christ! Yes, you may be the 'neck' as we say. You know, women say the head cannot turn with out the neck? While that is important, understand that it is the head that makes the decision to tell the neck to move in the first place!

Esther fasted and prayed and moved on the Word of God that was in her heart and spirit. She picked HER TIME, which had to be the Right Time to speak to her man in way that would influence him to save an entire race of people!

It was her time to show God that she learned the things He needed her to know about How to be a First Lady!

She was a lady who found herself in an orphanage lifestyle, yet won a pageant with no make up! She was a lady who was called to lead in a time when God was not even talking.

She was not a man; she was a first lady who had a responsibility to protect a nation. She was first of all, a lady who had to break a law and risk her life for a people she represented. She was a lady that had a stride in her faith walk that affected the world even today. She was a First a Lady. She was a Lady First. She was a woman of God who just happened to be a lady who leads!